Naked
&
Ashamed

Sheela Fields

Contents

Contents

Acknowledgments

I would like to thank all those who inspired and assisted me in writing this book. Your words of encouragement and prayer kept me attentive and motivated. I will forever be grateful for your help, patience, and support.

Introduction

What is the one thing that can destroy your life, your reputation, and your intimate relationships with others? The answer is sexual temptation and the compulsion to fulfill your fleshly desires. Sexual temptation is a subject that most people are afraid to talk about, yet it causes most spiritual and emotional distress.

The average person struggles with at least one sexual temptation that no one knows about and hopes that no one finds out. It's a hidden desire for transgression that can lay dormant for years until it is activated by the wrong condition. Whereas some have learned to hide their temptations well and not give into the lust of the moment, others have difficulty remaining steadfast and show their weaknesses as they fall into the trap of temptation. In either case, sexual temptation should not be overlooked but faced squarely, as people can use your weaknesses in this area to attack your character and hold you hostage with their malicious and defaming ways.

Why do we overlook and hide temptation even as many try desperately to release themselves from it? Why would someone who is living their best life allow one temptation to overtake them and bring them down? These questions have been a mystery for years, as we don't fully understand the power of temptation, and its force it has over humanity.

This book is not written to condemn you or to expose your secret sins. It is written for you specifically to find the riches in your struggle and to explore the subject of temptation and its root causes. As sexual creatures, we have a choice: control our urges or allow them to control us. If we ignore the signs of ungodly desires, we allow them to fester and grow, ultimately swelling into a humongous fog of temptation. We must know and learn a subject before we can have control over it and prevent it from transforming us.

As long as sex is continuously exploited on television and in music, it's easy to understand why temptation is an issue we all have to face. My question is: Why are we afraid to address sexual temptation at its root? Are we afraid to look beyond our natural urges and delve deeper into the mind which chooses a senseless form of gratification? What is it that makes us go into a mental funk and forget everything that we have strived for? Why have we allowed temptation to control our rational thoughts and allowed our sexual sins to run rampant? We should all have a desire to help not only those who are battling physical sickness but also those battling sexual sickness. Compulsive thoughts of sexual temptations are a form of sinful affliction that can sneak up on anyone. The temptation alone—to say nothing of giving in to such lustful urges—can suddenly cost you everything you have worked for.

Religion has taught sexual sufferers to smile and act like everything is okay. Never let them see you sweat. Always look blessed, even if you are hurting, and everything will be okay. The problem with this philosophy is that we are all sexual beings; at times, we will all have ungodly thoughts. Sometimes these thoughts may last for a moment, and other times they may last longer. It's only when we ignore our good thoughts and start listening to our dirty thoughts that we run into trouble. That's when we act out of character, with lustful imaginations transforming our minds and actions.

Spiritually mature minds know how to refrain from any type of offensive or sexual temptation by quickly isolating and evaluating those thoughts. Such individuals may think a dirty thought, but they are mature enough to know how to control their behaviors. Others who aren't as mature tend to react to their sexual temptations by aggressively expressing their thoughts outwardly to others. Either way, temptations can have a detrimental effect if you don't put them in check. Such temptations are like weeds—if not managed and pruned carefully, before you know it, they can grow wild. Once you dabble with sexual temptation, it takes on a life all its own and grows out of control, leaving you surrounded by moral decay and unable to fix the problem.

Sexual temptation respects no person, no sexual orientation, and no spiritual affiliation. We all have been enticed by something and said in our hearts, "I wonder what it would be like to be sexually involved with that person." For a split second, your mind created a daydream and an endless love that didn't exist. We create unrealistic thoughts and uncontrollable actions that we would love to fulfill in the moment, not realizing how one moment can bring a whole season of anguish into our lives.

All men and women have an inner sexual evil to battle. Mark 7:21-23 tells us: *"For from within, out of the heart of men, proceed evil thoughts, adulteries, fornications, murders, thefts, covetousness, wickedness, deceit, lasciviousness, an evil eye, blasphemy, pride, foolishness: All these evil things come from within, and defile the man."* Sexual evil and tempting thoughts come from within our hearts. It's what we have been thinking about and meditating on that comes from within. That is why you can talk to a stranger for several minutes and tell whether or not you want to stay in the conversation or sneak away. You can tell what is on a person's mind even if you have been talking only for a short period. Does he or she have good thoughts, or can we sense an enticing and alluring form of the evilness of their heart? We must decide whom we will let in our space and what is attaching itself to us.

How many great men have destroyed their lives by falling into conversations that led into temptation? One minute they're on top of the world, enjoying a life of success with no serious problems, but a single sexual thought, a slip in judgment, can infiltrate their minds and ruin their entire world. They find themselves trapped in a world of deceit and self-indulgence, unable to resist sexual temptations. If great men and women can be tempted and tested, what makes us think that we can escape the impulses and tricks of temptations?

When we are tempted, we lose our conscious way of thinking for a moment. Our minds battle forcibly in secret. We ask ourselves, "Should I? Should I?" Meanwhile, the Enemy says quietly, "Do it! Do it!" Two forces begin to battle for our attention and to win us to their side. Once we submit, we are no longer in control of ourselves—temptation has taken the reins. As temptation exerts its total control, we find ourselves in a level of unreality that takes a major effort to cast aside. At the time of submission, stopping is the last thought on our minds as we enjoy the moments of passion and secrecy. In this way, we allow our hidden passions to affect our lives for months and sometimes years.

Whether we are tempted to cheat on a spouse, to try unnatural sexual acts, or to entice someone else into sexual temptation, it is all the same. Temptation does not discriminate; it does not care what job or title you hold. In fact, the more money and power you have, the more delicious you look to the Tempter. The Tempter needs you to sink into a world of sin without thought so that he or she can have control.

Its force can manifest in many ways, but the goal is always the same: to devour you. It can slowly creep through your thoughts, or it can come through others, including people close to you. This force is so clever it can quickly thrust you into a new lifestyle that you never knew existed. Either way, it is a destroyer and does not care who it destroys or hurts. It is a greedy, lustful spirit that won't stop until you put your foot on it and crush it beneath you.

1st Corinthians 10:13 tells us: *"There hath no temptation taken you but such as is common to man: but God is faithful, who will not suffer you to be tempted above that ye are able; but will with the temptation also make a way to escape, that ye may be able to bear it."* Scripture reminds us that there is no temptation that has come upon us than what is common to humanity. In other words, we are tempted the same way as others are tempted; there is no trial that has not been faced by someone else.

We should not be surprised or caught off guard when we are confronted with sexual trials. Instead, we have to be vigilant and look for ways to change our situations. Don't waste time battling fruitlessly. We will not be tempted above what we are able to handle, as a way of escape will be always be provided. We must follow the guidance of the Word and not feel powerless if we want to escape temptation and live in liberty.

As we move forward, understand that you must not be scared to face yourself if you are struggling with sexual temptations, as we will all battle temptation in one form or another. Whether you are the victim or the tempter, there are many lessons that can be learned.

As we continue through the chapters of this book, we will journey through this controversial subject that we typically neglect or ignore. We will study biblical strategies that we can use to protect ourselves from this force that is always lurking, ready to take down the most steadfast and powerful among us.

So open up your hearts and get ready for this exciting journey as we travel through the Scriptures. Let's not let sexual temptation become a part of our lives and cause us to decline spiritually. Freedom means being free from all sexual bondage that the world throws our way. Remember: your deliverance depends on you and your ability to break free of all situations that will tempt you sexually and emotionally.

Let's put on spiritual armor and put sexual temptation in its place. It's time for us to move into honor and integrity and prepare for greater living. We must cease from any type of sexual immorality that will take us out of purpose.

Temptation is designed to trap us, but we can learn to avoid those pitfalls that are designed to keep us entangled in sexual sin, and stay in control.

CHAPTER 1

What Is Temptation?

Before we battle sexual temptation, we must first define it. Sexual temptation is an urge or desire to do something sexually immoral and pursue a thought that is impulsive or degrading. It involves looking at something that is sexually appetizing while weak and impulsively wanting a taste of it. Allowing your mind to "debate" whether you should take the forbidden fruit or leave it allows that temptation to occupy dangerous space in your mind. Although the sexual temptation itself might last only for a moment, one slip can turn it into a lifetime of disaster.

Temptation is cleverly designed to entice you sexually and pull you into a weakened state. Gratifying the flesh feels good, but never ends well. Once you fall into temptation, it could be years before you come back to your senses and break free. Only he whom the Son sets free is free indeed. Only Jesus can free you from sexual temptation and sin. Once that sin is embedded in you, you have entered its clutches and will have to strategically attack it.

You cannot be productive in life if you are constantly falling into temptation. Your behavior and actions tell all when you react to beauty or situations in a way that reveals your desires and impulses. By falling into the clutches of temptation and acting accordingly, you not only destroy a person's respect for you, but you will destroy the effectiveness of the message that you are trying to impart. Once a person has been tempted by you sexually, they lose all respect for you and will never perceive you in the same way.

We have all been tempted, and we each deal with such temptation in different ways. For example, someone in a drunken state may fall into temptation more quickly than someone who is sober. Someone lonely and repressed may fall into temptation a lot more easily than someone who has a busy and exciting life. Someone who is mentally unstable may fall into temptation more rapidly than someone who is mentally stable. No matter whom you are or what job title you hold, you will be tempted at some point. Temptation is that still, small voice that encourages you to satisfy the flesh—no matter how destructive that might be.

A nurse whom we will call Julie tells us her story; she was tempted to sleep with her neighbor's husband Jordan. Julie would spend her days flirting with Jordan as he did yard work; daydreaming of the time that she would have him. Julie kept up her flirting behavior for years until she finally propositioned Jordan and ended up having an affair.

Julie lost everything due to the sexual temptation that was lurking within her, suffering from dejection after her neighbor used and ignored her. In this situation, Julie was the tempter and dedicated years of her life to seducing someone who barely knew her.

The great Tempter, which we will discuss more in the

next chapter is designed to study you and doesn't bother alluring you with something that you don't like. He is careful to wait for the right moment in your weakness to shock you with the sexual enticement of something that you love or desire. Thus, it's obvious why temptation takes the form of something that you like to do or have an urge to do sexually.

James 1:14 tells us: *"But every man is tempted, when he is drawn away of his own lust and is enticed."* Temptation is a force that brings you down by drawing you away into your own lust. This comes through natural desires and emotions. Because we are sexual beings, temptations can come in different ways through various avenues. It might be through impulsive thoughts or fleeting urges that no one can see, or it might be through urges that we have been contemplating for a while. Regardless, there must be an unfulfilled desire in order for temptation to have the necessary power over us, to make us crave indulging in its pursuit. Temptation can also manifest through someone else who tries to tempt us into participating in their corrupt desires to fulfill their own inner lust.

There isn't much we can do in the moment when we are tempted and drawn away by our fleshly lust. We cannot see our actions clearly when we are so far gone mentally lusting after something. I am sure Julie, whom we met above, could not rationally examine herself and her behavior while she was in her lustful state. In the heat of the moment, she didn't care about what others saw. It was only later, when she had lost everything that she reflected on her situation and was surprised by her actions.

People who are sexually tempted do not set out to lose their way but are overtaken in the moment. After a temptation has been fed, your excitement and urge to continue feeding it often declines. In other words, when the temptation has been fulfilled, it temporarily loses its power and the urge to give in grows weaker.

A woman whom we will call Susan was struggling with a bout of depression after certain hard events in her life. After going months without counseling or help, Susan received a call from a man whom she hadn't heard from in years. He would listen to Susan's sob stories day after day and seemed genuinely concerned about her situation.

After he noticed that she was depressed, he began telling her how beautiful she used to be and started propositioning her for sex. Susan rejected him for months even though she felt sexually tempted. Finally, she gave into him in her depressive state and began having late date nights with him. After several months of using her for sex and mistreating her, he was gone. This story, sadly, is all too common. Susan was a perfect candidate for her tempter's lust. She blamed everyone but herself for falling into her lustful temptation of loneliness and desperation.

James 1:13 tells us: *"Let no man say when he is tempted, I am tempted of God: for God cannot be tempted with evil, neither tempteth. He any man."* So, we first know that temptation is never from God, and based on Scripture, temptation is considered evil. We are warned strongly that we should not speak certain heresies about temptation.

For instance, there are those who think that temptation

is good because it boosts the morale of the person being tempted and makes them feel good about themselves, but we should never be fooled or sidetracked by temptation. We should always maintain our focus on doing the right thing, rather than struggling to do the wrong things.

We should always be conscious of our surroundings and ready when temptation comes. Temptation is insidious. It is a mental process that often catches you off guard, inserts a thought of need, and causes you to misinterpret the situation at hand.

Although we can also be tempted to steal, lie, and do other sinful things, sexual temptation is particularly harmful because it involves your body, soul, and spirit. It's different from other temptations because it also involves other people and affects many areas of our lives. As we explore the body, soul, and spirit, we will see the effects sexual temptation has on us and the surrounding environment.

Your body sends messages to your mind and you often envision yourself being intimate with your tempter, causing you to battle your own thoughts. The idea of someone touching and caressing your body can send you into a tailspin of pleasurable and raunchy thoughts. Not thinking rationally about your situation pushes you out of reality and leads you to test the waters of temptation. It can trap you in a world of desires you cannot easily escape. The tempter wants you to make a quick, irrational decision to get involved and, depending on your circumstances, your flesh can be weak and lead you right into a dangerous desire.

Your soul is affected as you go through emotional mental battles over what is right and what is wrong. The intimate source of your soul has already imagined the course of these events; it sits and waits for you to make the decision not to fall. Your soul is forced to keep your intimate thoughts secret and present an outward mask of smiles designed to keep you in bondage. Out of nowhere, your emotional thoughts can pop up, presenting you with an imaginary scene that forces you to dream about the good feelings and excitement that could come from your seductive temptation. Your soul has a lot of hidden emotions that can lay dormant, then overcome you at a moment's notice.

Your spirit too, suffers from the trials of temptation. If we are not careful and not filled with truth, we will have a treacherous time trying to escape temptation. Our spirit may know the truth, but if our bodies and minds don't follow through, we will make an unwise choice and fall. Your spirit is always trying to follow the right path, but we often ignore our spirit's wise guidance—especially when we are enjoying our tempting thoughts and looking for a reason to dive into sin. Our spirit must be fed daily so we can have strength in our times of trouble.

As we look at our body, soul, and spirit, we can conclude that we all can be tempted—and we can all be tempters. No one is exempt. You can encounter an unexpected enticement that looks so inviting that it would be hard to resist. Temptation is like eating a cake everyday only to find that soon, you have developed diabetes. We enjoy the taste, but do not account for the effects of the sugar. If we allow ourselves to ignore temptation and function like it does not exist, it won't be long before we will be tried in that area. Whether we pass the test depends upon our knowledge of what is going on spiritually and physically.

As we move into chapter two, recognizing the Tempter, let's keep in mind the different examples of how sexual temptation can take on many forms. Temptation does not take a single form, but many, as we are all different and have different ideologies. Daily, we must stay alert in all we do so we do not become victims of temptation or a tempter to someone else.

CHAPTER 2

Recognizing the Tempter

A tempter is someone who entices you by flesh or words into a lustful state of desire as a way to control you sexually. You will never know when or from where a tempter will come. It could be someone close to your family, someone who has known you for years, an enemy, or even a friend.

A tempter can be a male or a female. The tempter is always looking for someone he can devour as quickly as possible. He seeks someone who will fall into sexual temptation without thinking. He knows if you think too long about it, you may come to your senses and not fall for his tricks. To trap you, he keeps you in suspense and off guard. It's like a sport to the tempter as he starts with a simple act to entice you. Something as small as a wink, can set sexual temptation in motion. The tempter tries to create a connection to you so he can lead you astray. Once you indicate you have fallen, that's it. He is in control.

When the flesh is weak, the tempter will strike, embarking on a mission to control you based on your own weaknesses and desires. He or she thinks he knows what you like and feeds off that vulnerability. His aim is to grab you in your weakest state and use you for his own purposes. The tempter never considers your life and the effects he will have on you. He is selfish and greedy and does not care about the evil and torment he will bring. The tempter doesn't care if you have a mate, children, or a ministry. His goal is to bind you to him.

Although the tempter may watch you and sense what you like, he still does not know your desires. The tempter issues smooth enticements to see your reaction. If you react excitably, he keeps the temptation going until he has you. Once he has your heart involved in the lascivious activity, then you have to succumb to the tempter. After falling for the tempter, your catastrophe begins.

You must stop the tempter in his tracks by ignoring or verbally resisting his advances. When he or she flirts and make suggestive moves, this is the time to back out. The longer you engage, the more involved and intertwined you become.

Your lifestyle and emotional condition affects how you will handle your temptation. For example, if you suffer from loneliness, you need to be extra alert for temptation, keeping your flesh in order during your test.

Again, the tempter may use a slow process, challenging you with small things just to see how you react. If you appear interested, he starts tempting you with bigger things. The tempter watches slowly as you fall into a lustful state, easy to control. Therefore, never react to temptation! In particular, don't give in to what you see with your naked eyes. Temptation can appear as nice muscles, a great body, or beautiful skin. These attributes can present a false sense of what is really there—those beautiful features may hide a dark heart of immorality and sin.

Falling prey to small temptations can lead to larger trials as you are tossed back and forth by your urges and your tempters. We all know someone who has a different mate every week. They are constantly getting hurt and used by individuals. Anyone who tempts them can get a piece of the pie. Tempters are wise in choosing weak prey. These are individuals who spend their life tempting and enticing unsuspecting individuals into submission, only to move on to the next person. They love disastrous relationships because they know that their commitment will not be for long.

Tempters are not only present in your social life; they can also be at your place of employment. There are people who become tempters in order to get favors and promotions. They feel the need to exploit the weakness of those in charge just to get an edge over others. These individuals entice their bosses and use several methods to tempt those in authority. They believe that if they can control the boss sexually, they can control the entire workplace. They tempt those with power because they are not sure that their talent is enough to achieve their goals of moving ahead.

This type of temptation is dangerous as tempters spend more time trying to control people with sex and lies than they do putting their talent forward. Many who have gone that route often tell of their failures, as using this method of sexual enticement often is unsuccessful in the long run.

A woman whom we will call Tammy is an example of someone who was caught in a scandal of temptation.

Tammy was always the outcast at the office and fought to get closer and more involved with the other employees. One day while typing, Tammy overheard her boss talking about going to a club outside the city for ladies' night. In her desperation and desires, Tammy went home early, dressed up in tight clothes, and put on extensive make up. She showed up at the club that her boss spoke of, meeting and greeting people; coworkers assumed that she was a regular there.

Tammy spent the entire night flirting with the boss and making comments to entice him. After several drinks, Tammy got drunk and began taking her clothes off. Tammy woke up in her boss's bed, not knowing what happened to her. The next day, her boss, whom she enticed all night, avoided her and then disrespected her in front of the other employees. Tammy had to eventually quit her job due to her embarrassment.

Here, Tammy was the tempter. Although she may have been violated, she was too ashamed to say a thing. The same person Tammy tempted used her. The tables were turned, and she was the one who paid the price for her actions. Like Tammy, anytime you tempt someone, be ready for the price you may have to pay. Tammy spent years worrying about what could have happened to her and had to live each day wondering why the boss suddenly hated her. Tammy's embarrassment and ultimate fall lasted for years.

Matthew 26:41 tells us: *"Watch and pray that ye enter not into temptation: the spirit indeed is willing, but the flesh is weak."* Even though our spirits are willing to do the right things, we all have weak flesh. The flesh is that human part of us that likes to be touched and pampered. When we are dealing with weak flesh, we must be careful that we don't follow after its cravings and start desiring the things of the flesh. Temptation is drawn through the flesh and the flesh does not stop. The more the flesh sees, the more the flesh desires. We can become enemies to ourselves by allowing our flesh to dictate our every move. When something enticing comes along and takes us out of our routine, our flesh rises up and can be forcefully distracting if not controlled.

Before we move into the next chapter, "The Naked Truth," let's recall from this chapter that anyone can be a tempter—even you. Those close to you can be tempters, just as those who only know you through association can be tempters.

Just because someone is a close friend or a business associate does not mean they will not be tempters. The only purpose of the tempter is to get you to fall into a web of seduction. So be careful of who you allow in your daily space and always be conscious of people's intentions. Keep your environment safe and in control, so you can resist what the tempter is bringing to you.

CHAPTER 3

The Naked Truth

When we think of the word "naked," we think of someone or something without clothing. Being naked is not natural for us, so we sometimes feel uncomfortable or self-conscious when we find ourselves bare. Nakedness means that everyone will see every part of our being, and see what we are really made of.

Spiritually speaking, if someone were to strip down your thoughts until you were naked, would they be surprised by what they'd see? Of course, some of your thoughts would not be pure, as we all struggle with bad thoughts. Such thoughts are always hidden because we dare not to show our deep sexual thoughts.

Like wearing clothing, we cover our innermost thoughts with smiles and laughs to impress others. If we are covering feelings and emotions with outer expressions, we think no one will ever know the truth about our thoughts. We like it this way because we can lust, desire, and fulfill our sexual appetites and no one will ever know.

Yes, Christians can lust and have sexual appetites even though we act like we don't. We have a hard time believing that some Christians aren't perfect. As soon as they are caught in sin, we act like we are surprised by their actions. No one should ever be surprised by any sin that is committed by anyone. The Enemy preys on our filthy thoughts and attacks us in areas where we are weak. He knows that we have weak spots, and he continually searches for those hidden temptations.

If he sees that we like certain sexual activities, he will make sure that we are tempted with them, often catching us off guard in our times of weakness. If he gets a clue to those vulnerable spots in your spiritual life, he will entice you as long as you are bare and not clothed spiritually.

We must understand that we are all capable of sin and should examine ourselves if we're tempted. Spiritual nakedness is important because we can learn about ourselves instead of being afraid of what we find. Yet this can be painful, as some temptations and sins have been with us for years. Understanding why we have carried that specific temptation for so long is the key to finding answers and remaining strong and steadfast. We must strive to understand ourselves and know that the battle comes from within. Just like removing old clothing, we must remove all of our excuses and justifications and return to the root cause of our desires.

Therefore, when you pray, you should be honest with yourself and expose your feelings, your sins, and everything that troubles you. Yes, even those sins you fight sexually. This is one way you can be real and expose the naked truth about what lies within to receive forgiveness.

Being open and truthful with yourself will settle your mind so you can be free from tempting thoughts. Don't be afraid to let loose in prayer and expose your dirty thoughts and constant temptations. Don't believe that you are troubled and useless because you may struggle with sexual temptations. If you honestly confess and yearn to get better, then you're on the right track for deliverance. Getting upset with yourself and allowing the Enemy to remind you constantly of your devilish behavior will never free you, as you will stay in condemnation.

Isaiah 64:6 tells us: *"But we are all as an unclean thing, and all our righteousness is as filthy rags, and we all fade as a leaf; and our iniquities, like the wind, have taken us away."* If we're not careful, our sins will turn into iniquities and we will label sin as right. This is how we can live in sin for years and never have a clue that we're doing so. Scripture tells us that we will never be perfect as long as we are on this earth. Thus, we should not be surprised when we struggle with sinful thoughts and behavior—the battle is constantly before us.

But there is a way forward. As soon as the bad thoughts come, we must be wise and not let them overtake us. Worrying about negative thoughts and blaming ourselves for them puts us on a path to self-hate. Using spiritual techniques such as prayer, fasting, and meditating on God's Word will give us answers.

A man whom we will call Sammie had his round of temptation in exposing his nakedness. Sammie first found himself tempted to watch pornographic movies when he was bored on the weekends. After years of being affected by his habit, Sammie was afraid that the movies were taking over his life. One way he combated these feeling was reading the Bible. Romans 12:2 tells us: *"And be not conformed to this world: but be ye transformed by the renewing of your mind, that ye may prove what is that good, and acceptable and perfect will of God."* Sammie knew that he had to do something drastic to counter his temptations. To combat his appetite for sexual movies, Sammie recited this Scripture so much that he literally didn't have time to watch them. His thoughts and appetite for the movies got weaker as he quoted and meditated on this same Scripture repeatedly. As the thoughts weakened, Sammie was able to replace his appetite for pornographic movies for more acceptable hobbies like reading and golf.

Stripping yourself down spiritually takes time and requires being real and honest with yourself. As Sammie's experience shows, it is not easy to destroy all of your filthy and tempting thoughts. Sammie knew that the Holy Scriptures would be helpful to him because of the power of Word. He knew he had to apply the Scriptures over and over to get the taste of the movies out of his soul. His attitude and determination to apply constant force against his sin helped his healing process.

The key is to identify your sinful thoughts, work on them, and have a desire to be healed. Tempting thoughts, which lead you into sin, are like having a small cut. If you don't put ointment on it and take care of it, it will become painful and get larger.

Just like a small cut, if you don't take care of your little thoughts, they can become big sores. You must do something about all those little thoughts, which can eventually become big and powerful thoughts. Be proactive in treating the small thoughts, because once you allow a small thought to become a sore, it takes considerable time and medicine to heal it. Mental sores can take months to heal, as you must get inside for transformation and healing.

In closing, we must stay focused and ready for temptation, constantly striving to be free of your sinful thoughts. We find the naked truth when we make a conscious effort to examine ourselves by stripping our thoughts all the way down to the core. When we take the time to examine ourselves, we are more apt to find a cure for our ailment and begin the healing process. This allows us to search ourselves spiritually. Always remember that we are responsible for our thoughts and actions and we must analyze ourselves to be effective in all areas of our lives.

CHAPTER 4

Our Sinful Nature

We often talks about sin, but what exactly *is* sin? Sin is an immoral act considered to be a transgression against a divine law. Sin goes all the way back to Adam and Eve in the first Book of the Bible. Genesis 2:16-17 tells us: *"And the Lord God commanded the man saying, of every tree of the garden thou mayest freely eat. But of the tree of the knowledge of good and evil, thou shalt not eat of it: for in the day that thou eatest thereof thou shalt surely die."*

Adam disobeyed this commandment, as Genesis 3:6 tells us. *"And when the woman saw that the tree was good for food and that it was pleasant to the eyes, and a tree to be desired to make one wise, she took of the fruit thereof, and did eat, and gave also unto her husband with her; and he did eat."* Before eating the forbidden fruit, we had a perfect world. However, after Adam disobeyed God due to the temptation fall of his wife, sin entered into us. There is nothing that we can do, as we are all born into sin.

Romans 7:19-20 tells us: *"For the good that I would I do not; but the evil which I would not, that I do. Now if I do that I would not, it is no more I that do it, but sin that dwelleth in me."* Our minds automatically open the door for sin due to the sin already seeded within us. We need to fight against sinful thoughts and reject sinful actions. We start with the right intentions, meaning to do the right things, but even the best of us can get caught up in all the wrong things.

How many of us go to work with the intention of saving the lost and doing the right thing? But then we find ourselves arguing with customers and even falling into compromising positions. The Apostle Paul said it best when he told us that we try to do right, only to find ourselves doing wrong.

Romans 3:23 tells us: *"For all have sinned and come short of the glory of God."* There is no person on this earth who does not sin and does not have areas in their life in which they struggle. Therefore, we should not look down on others who are in sin and judge them. We should be able to go to sinners with sincere concern and help them in their dilemma. Of course, some people don't want to get out of their sin—but that should not stop us. Planting that seed of encouragement will be remembered and appreciated when that person is finally ready to change, break free of their transgressions, and is liberated.

Proverbs 28:13 tells us: *"He that covereth his sins shall not prosper; but whoso confesseth and forsaketh them shall have mercy."* When we sin, our natural tendency is to conceal it. We like to hide under the sheets, so that Heaven won't see us. We're like Adam and Eve who sewed fig leaves together and made loin coverings; we cover our nakedness, as we discussed in the previous chapter. We enjoy and cover our sins until we are caught or exposed.

However, in our sunken state of sin, we should always be conscious that it *is* a sin and confess it. Sneaking around and hiding our sin only brings condemnation and guilt.

Only when we earnestly confess our sins can we expect to experience mercy and, in turn, can we find the Advocate who will show us compassion.

Psalms 32:3-5 states: *"When I kept silence, my bones waxed old through my rearing all the day long. For day and night thy hand was heavy upon me: my moisture is turned into the drought of the summer. (Selah). I acknowledged my sin unto thee and mine iniquity have I not hid. I said, I will confess my transgressions unto the Lord; and thou forgavest the iniquity of my sin. (Selah)."* Confession is the only way to go if you are serious about turning the tide of your sins. If you hold on to your sins and worry about others finding out about them, your bones will wax old— that is, you will feel the effects of your sin.

Some think if they pray and fast long enough, their sinful thoughts will just disappear. This is untrue. It doesn't matter how long you pray or how long you fast; you will still sin. Sin is something we are born with—that is why we must confess it.

We learn from David in Psalms 51:4-5: *"Against thee, thee only, have I sinned, and done this evil in thy sight; that thou mightest be justified when thou speakest and be clear when thou judgest. Behold I was shapen in iniquity; and in sin did my mother conceive me."* When we sin, we not only hurt ourselves, we go against the Creator. This is why we must get serious about sin and not let it fester and grow bigger. We are quick to look at our neighbor's sin and judge them. But really, we must take a personal inventory and clean up our own sins.

Once we realize that we were born into sin, we can understand that our sinful nature will always be there.

Some think we are born perfect, that we learn sin and corrupt our lives. As we see in the Bible, however, sin was born in Adam and Eve when they disobeyed. Therefore, we should not be so hard on ourselves when we fall into sinful thoughts or fall into temptation. Jesus knew that we would all be born in sin and would have a hard time living our lives in holy perfection. That is the reason he came to die for us.

John 19:30 tells us: *"When Jesus, therefore, had received the vinegar, he said, it is finished: and he bowed his head and gave up the ghost."* It is clear that Jesus knew the inherent nature of sin in mankind—every person born on earth will have a problem with sin. Yet that is why he died for us; in this passage, "it is finished" means he has absolved all the believers' sins from the Cross. If you truly believe in your heart that he is the Christ and He died for you, and if you confess your sins earnestly, you will receive mercy and forgiveness.

Hebrews 8:12 tells us: *"For I will be merciful to their unrighteousness, and their sins and their iniquities will I remember no more."* Isn't it wonderful that our sins and iniquities will be remembered no more? But we must confess our sins with a pure heart and believe that our sins have been forgiven. We must be honest and transparent.

Too many of us refuse to do this. We stay condemned and ashamed, feeling that we are not good for the world if we have sinned sexually. We make excuses for our sinful behavior and even convince ourselves that our actions are all right.

A good example of this is someone saying, "In the moment, I was weak." There is no such thing as "in the moment." As much as we want to believe that everything happens in the moment, it does not. The sin was already in you, waiting for a chance to be released. When the environment is ripe and the atmosphere is right, we can all sin. It is not "the moment" that puts you at a disadvantage because the sin is already within you. Temptation is always there; sin is always there. "The moment" is merely when we seize the opportunity and allow the sin to multiply and abound.

That is why we must be extra careful when we put ourselves in compromising positions, especially when we're unsure of the other person's motives. Some examples of this are date rapes and sexual attacks. These individuals who endure such events have suffered because of the sins indwelling in the minds of those who cannot control their sinful nature.

The world is full of sin and sinful acts. When we turn on the radio, we hear sinful music filled with cursing and all kinds of degrading lyrics. When we turn on the television, there are more and more sinful shows being broadcast. When we look on the internet, we are bombarded with sinful imagery. Pornography is one of the biggest businesses in the world. This tells us that it is not only worldly people who are into sexual sin—believers are as well.

Unfortunately, your sin is not going anywhere. It does not matter how long your church dress is, or how fine your church suit is, you will still have sin. You might be doing well, walking the path of truth, and suddenly think of a sin committed ten years ago. The Enemy never lets you forget, especially if you are trying to live right and help others in the faith.

A gentleman whom we will call Mendez learned the hard way about the consequences of sin. After previously working for a large firm in New York, Mendez came into his new company with a good attitude. He had set his mind not to date on the job and to always maintain a professional demeanor.

After two years of working at his new company, Mendez was excited to find that he was next in line for a promotion that two other people also wanted. While waiting on his promotion, he learned that the company had hired a new secretary, whom we will call Maxine, who spoke Spanish and French. Spanish was Mendez's first language; so naturally, he was excited that someone could now understand him in his native language.

From time to time, throughout her first months on the job, Maxine would speak to Mendez in Spanish. He thought nothing of it and simply assumed that Maxine liked to speak Spanish. As time went on, Maxine flirted with Mendez in Spanish and always told him to keep it a secret.

\After a year, Maxine took her flirting even further. She propositioned Mendez to meet her at a restaurant in another town, thirty miles away. Mendez took the bait, as he was getting anxious while waiting on his possible promotion. Their meetings became regular and intense. After meeting with Maxine at the restaurant several times a week for some time, Mendez came to trust her and began to share all his personal struggles on the job. After learning

Mendez's most intimate secrets, Maxine the tempter was ready to strike.

One night, Maxine took it further and kissed Mendez, groping him and telling him how handsome he was. Mendez had suspected this would happen eventually, but trusted Maxine, since she had never revealed anything he shared. Instead of resisting, Mendez—being weak and tempted—took Maxine to his house, had sex with her, and allowed her to spend the night. The next morning, though, Maxine was nowhere to be found.

When Mendez reported to work, his coworkers met him at his car to give him goodbye condolences. Because Mendez did not know what was going on, he asked to speak to his supervisor. He learned that he had been fired for sleeping with a coworker on the job, which was prohibited by the company bylaws. Not only was he unaware that was a rule, but he also did not know Maxine was married.

Two years after Mendez was fired, he ran into Maxine at a warehouse in the same city. Maxine apologized to him and seemed disturbed about something as they spoke. She told Mendez that she had been paid a thousand dollars to entice him into sleeping with her as a way to get him fired. She explained that several of his coworkers were upset with him because he was next in line for a promotion, and they concocted a plan to get rid of him. She explained that her entire engagement with the company was only to tempt him and get him to fall into sexual sin.

After this, Mendez could never get his life back on track; he trusted no one at any of his jobs due to his betrayal.

Although most temptations do not end this way, you can see that Mendez knew in his heart he would eventually be tempted. He started off well, but temptation kept nudging at him. Instead of nipping it in the bud, though, he allowed the temptation to keep growing until it manifested and caused him to fall in spectacular fashion.

This entire story shows us we can have good intentions, but still get caught up in sexual temptation. If Mendez could have stopped and really looked at what was going on, he might have been able to see the clues that were present about his enemies' plans. Maxine arrived at the time of his expected promotion, immediately took notice of him, and tempted him with appealing interactions and sweet words. We must be aware of such temptations and tempters in our lives and always question their motivations.

As we go throughout our daily lives, we must also be conscious of our sins, fighting hard not to allow sin to take over or cause other ailments to come upon us. David said in Psalms 51:3: *"For I acknowledge my transgressions: and my sin is ever before me."* Although our sin is ever before us, we should not let sin take over our lives or cause us to live a life of misery and shame.

Every day we have an opportunity to sin with something. We must all strive to keep ourselves motivated to live upright. Praying, fasting, and reading the Word are several ways we can combat our inherent sin. Being responsible for yourself and remaining vigilant in your thoughts and actions should be something you strive for daily. Sin can take you all the way down to rock bottom and can bring on stress and spiritual sickness; it can even have you hiding and sneaking throughout the day.

Make it simple: realize that sin is what Jesus died for and we should be thankful that He nailed all our sins on the Cross. We should attempt to live in an upright manner, and should we fall, we should repent and know that Jesus said in 1st John 1:9: *"If we confess our sins, he is faithful and just to forgive us our sins, and to cleanse us from all unrighteousness."* Thus, if we get caught up in sin, we should confess and know that our sins are forgiven.

Always remember that Jesus paid a heavy price, and He already knows what you and I did and what we will do. When we confess our sins, the cleansing begins. We cannot be afraid to address our sins and know that Jesus is available to us. Thank God; He forgives us in our faults and does not condemn us in our sins.

CHAPTER 5

Toxic Thoughts

To get a good understanding of this chapter, let's first define the word "toxic." Toxic means dangerous, deadly, or poisonous. The next word in the chapter title is "thoughts." Thoughts refer to an impression, an opinion, or a reflection. When both words are placed together, we have the phrase "toxic thoughts"—opinions or impressions which are deadly or poisonous.

We must be conscious of our toxic thoughts because if we live in sin, we will always have them. Thoughts that arise unannounced, uninvited, and have no business in our minds. They are designed to strip away our focus and divert us from progress. How many relationships have we damaged or destroyed by following toxic thoughts? We build close relationships, only to follow a toxic thought that derails everything. Once a thought is expressed or spoken, it becomes a reality and changes our situation. That is why we must be careful about all our thoughts— even the thoughts we entertain about ourselves.

Joshua 1:8 tells us: *"The book of the law shall not depart out of thy mouth, but thou shalt meditate therein day and night that thou mayest observe to do according to all that is written therein: for then thou shalt make thy way prosperous and then thou shalt have good success."* We are clearly told that the only way to refocus toxic thoughts is to read the Book of the Law and meditate on it day and night. This does not mean that you will not have toxic thoughts; rather, as you read the Word, you will become prepared and ready for unwanted thoughts.

As we meditate on certain Scriptures, that Scripture will be written on our hearts. When a Scripture is written on your heart, it is like a light on your path that shines on negative thoughts that come to distract you. Keep the Word with you so you won't be deceived when a toxic thought appears; use it to shine a light of truth and keep you on the righteous path.

Toxic thoughts are insidious; they often strike at times of enjoyment. Have you ever been excited about a change in your life, such as an engagement or great opportunity, only to find yourself thinking about an old disappointment that left you upset? That toxic thought appeared in an attempt to infiltrate your time of joy. This is why 2nd Corinthians 10:5 tells us: *"Casting down imaginations, and every high thing that exalteth itself against the knowledge of God and bringing into captivity every thought to the obedience of Christ."* These instructions out of Corinthians help us to recognize thoughts can rise up, trying to overwhelm our sure and certain knowledge.

Scripture tells us that we must take captive every thought that comes into our minds. If we allow our thoughts to run rampant, then we will lose our sense of control and start steering our lives in the wrong direction. What we do with incoming thoughts determines the direction of our lives.

If we allow our toxic thoughts to take over, then we allow ourselves to dwell in trouble and open ourselves up for strife and unnecessary pain. If you entertain toxic thoughts, they will get worse and eventually sweep you off course. But if you take charge, you will find that the Word and your faith allow you to rebuke and change your thoughts.

Toxic thoughts can affect our hearts as well. Jeremiah 17:9 tells us: *"The heart is deceitful above all things, and desperately wicked; who can know it."* Many of our toxic thoughts come from the heart or our inner being. Have you ever spoken with someone and suddenly get a crazy idea about that person or something they may have done? The conversation had nothing to do with the thought, but you start seeing their old temptations and suspecting their sins. When you meet someone for the first time, are you finding the good in the person or searching for something bad? We cannot escape the daily fight between good and evil.

What we open our hearts and minds to can also affect the way we entertain toxic thoughts. The more we watch filth and accept what we see, the more we start thinking and acting like the filth we watch. You may think that enjoying an occasional filthy movie or filthy conversation is okay, but the more we entertain these types of activities, the more our hearts are desensitized to it. We start opening up our minds to stronger indecency, only to find ourselves feeling comfortable with anything and everything we see or hear.

Have you ever played a song full of cursing repeatedly? Eventually, you will find yourself singing the song out of nowhere at an event, cussing right along with the song.

This is because you have allowed that song and its lyrics to get into your heart. It sat long enough to fester and wait for the right moment for your weakness to be revealed. Even years later, you may find yourself singing that same song out of nowhere, remembering all the filthy lyrics and cuss words. That is how deep-rooted small toxic thoughts can be.

Another example of a toxic thought involves children who have been told from a very young age that they will never be anything and should never try. Hearing those words can deeply affect a child, sitting in their young mind and festering with time. That child may find himself having a hard time as an adult, all from the influence of that toxic thought that came from a toxic statement. Therefore, we should always speak words of encouragement and life to children and others who are struggling.

We have all had some toxic words spoken around us in one form or another. Thus, we should not be judgmental of others who have not yet fulfilled their full potential. You never know what it took for someone to get where they are, and the pain they suffered to get there.

Proverbs 4:23 tells us: *"Keep thy heart with all diligence; for out of it are the issues of life."* As we learned earlier, there are various connections between the heart and life issues. For us to keep control of our toxic thoughts, we must take control of our hearts. When you are around negative people daily and you converse with them and get involved emotionally in their lives, it influences you. For example, let's take someone who has just had their heart broken. Most people with broken hearts do not think rationally.

They are doing things out of the ordinary, controlled by their pain and toxic thoughts. "If only I had done better! "If I only treated him right! They constantly blame themselves for their broken heart. But this isn't a reasonable way of thinking.

If someone can get control of your heart, then they have you. How many women have fallen in love with a man whom they barely knew, only to discover that he only wanted one thing and never had the right intentions in the first place? Instead of moving on, the woman's heart is filled with so much pain and such toxic thoughts that her behavior often becomes evil. She finds herself doing unusual things to hurt him and acting out of character. A heart enduring much pain can turn you into an unrecognizable person. A person even you don't know.

A woman whom we will call Jenny had a battle with her toxic thoughts. Jenny worked in a ministry as a secretary and also worked part-time as a records clerk. While at her part-time job, Jenny would sit around and gossip, listening to several people who made it their mission to make trouble at work. After listening to her toxic coworkers at that job for more than a year, Jenny began to bring her behavior from her records clerk job to her church job.

While doing her secretarial duties at church, Jenny found herself gossiping and slandering people in the church. Her voice would get loud as she started making accusations against leadership figures, complaining that they were not doing enough work. She even took it upon herself to investigate people's criminal history while looking over church records.

It wasn't until a coworker at the church approached Jenny and told of her behavior that she realized her toxic thoughts from her clerical position had entered her ministry job. Jenny said she had no conscious knowledge of her behavior and immediately made sure to be cautious whenever speaking about certain subjects concerning the church.

Perhaps you are like Jenny, gossiping and starting trouble without knowing where your behavior originated. Although pain causes the majority of toxic thoughts towards others, there are other ways that you can develop toxic thoughts.

Being around people who speak toxically and act toxic can cause you to act similarly. Being in a toxic environment can sneak up on you; before you know it, you too are engaged in toxic thinking and doing the same toxic things. This is why keeping the right company helps you free yourself from negativity.

The Bible says in Philippians 4:8: *"Finally, brethren, whatsoever things are true, whatsoever things are honest, whatsoever things are just, whatsoever things are pure, whatsoever things are lovely, whatsoever things are of a good report; if there be any virtue, and if there be any praise, think on these things."* The Bible teaches us that we must always think about good and pure things. This can be hard as we live our daily lives and are confronted with people who act toxic toward us and don't care. But we must stay the course and remain in control of our thoughts and actions, as we are expected to behave better.

With all the sexual industries throughout society and all the demonic television shows that people love to watch, it is becoming harder to concentrate on good things. You cannot drive to a restaurant without seeing a sexualized sign or an ad trying to recruit you into buying something indecent. That is why you must be responsible for thinking on good things and filling your spirit with the Word.

We must keep in mind that we are responsible for our toxic thoughts and expected to conduct ourselves in a manner that is good. No one can control your thoughts and words other than you. There is no school or anonymous program that is going to teach you how to tame your thoughts and words. The best way to control your toxic thoughts is to meditate on the Word and always be conscious of what you are saying to others and how they may perceive your words.

If a toxic thought comes to you, learn how to let it go and keep moving in a positive way. There is no excuse for us to allow toxic thoughts to run rampant and take control. Of course, it takes practice to refocus thoughts, but we have the best textbook available: the Bible.

CHAPTER 6

Recognizing Weaknesses

Weakness is defined as lacking strength or ability. Let's face it: we all have weaknesses, as there is not a perfect person on this earth. That is why you should never worship anyone or anything other than the God of Abraham, Isaac, and Jacob. How many of us have worshipped movie stars and musicians only to find that their lives are more messed up than ours? When we realize that they are only human, the power they have over us disappears and they become regular people.

Many people have been damaged by overrating people and putting them on high pedestals only to find that they suffer just like the rest of us. If the truth is told, average citizens tend to handle their weaknesses a lot better than those we incorrectly idolize. Some of us started babying our weaknesses from childhood and brought them into adulthood with us. Some of us cultivated our weaknesses later in life, building on experiences we've had as adults. No matter when or how your weakness came upon you, you should be able to recognize your weaknesses and strive to get stronger.

Weakness should not overpower you and leave you feeling ashamed. Instead of waiting for our weaknesses to be exposed, we should face them and take responsibility for them. Although we may not be the author of our weakness, we are still the ones living with it. It is our responsibility to check ourselves, remain true to ourselves, and face everything that has us bound, and fight to get tough.

Sometimes we have to drive our weakness out and stand strong against it. We can find strength in Isaiah 40:29, which tells us: *He giveth power to the faint, and to them that have no might he increaseth strength.* " Isn't it great to know that when we have no might, we are increased in strength? We no longer have to hide our weaknesses and live in fear. It's only when we are true to ourselves and able to expose our weaknesses that we can allow healing to come.

I am reminded of a woman whom we will call Terri who had a bout with weakness. Terri had to live perfectly all her life in order to survive in her household. Her mother and father were prominent people in their city, and she had to carry herself like an adult when she was a child. She was greeting people and smiling when necessary, like a puppet controlled by her environment; she performed as expected all the time.

As Terri got older, she realized that she had a hard time relating to people on a natural level. She never got to know herself, so when she tried to make friends, it was hard for her to connect and hold a normal conversation. She continued trying to be perfect, but no one understood her intentions.

One day while on a date, Terri met a man whom we will call Tim. Tim made a comment to her, asking, "Are you a plus size?" This one statement sent Terri on an emotional journey that would last five years. Terrified of not being perfect, Terri constantly looked at herself in the mirror and was always revisiting what Tim said.

She became bulimic, trying to lose weight and escape the stigma of being plus size. Plus size was not the "perfect" weight for her height, so she became depressed after she could not lose the weight. Terri never told anyone how emotionally upsetting and draining it was for her to feel imperfect. After several months, Terri became sick due to her disordered eating and spent weeks in the hospital recovering.

Terri's weakness was always trying to be perfect. Being around two parents who expected her to be perfect all the time made her feel like she had to live her entire life flawlessly. Later in life, all it took was one person criticizing her to begin a downward path of self-mutilation.

Hebrews 4:15-16 tells us: *"For we have not a high priest which cannot be touched with the feeling of our infirmities; but was in all points tempted like as we are yet without sin. Let us, therefore, come boldly unto the throne of grace that we may obtain mercy, and find grace to help in time of need."* Our high priest Jesus is able to sympathize with all of our weaknesses. He has been tempted, but yet He is without sin. We should be thankful for the Cross, because he bore all of our weaknesses. We should not be embarrassed about our mistakes in life because we have a God we can go to that has been through everything that we have. He knew what we would face, yet has made a way for us to have grace in our time of need. Jesus sympathizes with us and all of our weaknesses. Trying to hide our weaknesses only makes our lives resentful and harder.

Because we are all made differently and all have been in different environments, we are each weak in distinct areas. One person's weakness may be fleshly things, such as lust and sex. Another person's weakness may be food and drink.

Some of us were blind to our weaknesses until we were confronted with them. For example, divorce makes some realize how weak they are. They never knew they had weaknesses until they were faced with a situation that they had no control over. Some people suffer emotional breakdowns and health issues after divorce. This does not make them less of a person, but such situations can reveal powerlessness and show how much we need Jesus. The peace of God is what gets many through their most difficult situations.

In 2nd Corinthians 12:9-10, we are told: *"And he said unto me, my grace is sufficient for thee: for my strength is made perfect in weakness. Most gladly therefore will I rather glory in my infirmities that the power of Christ may rest upon me. Therefore, I take pleasure in infirmities, in reproaches, in necessities, in persecutions in distresses for Christ's sake: for when I am weak, then I am I strong."* Strength is made perfect in weakness because there is no pride and arrogance in weakness. In your weakness, you fully submit, because you cannot fix the area of your weakness on your own. These verses will keep you motivated when you are struggling in weakness.

Know that when you are weak, you are strong. This statement must be perceived in the Spirit, because when you are weak, you never see yourself as strong—but when you stand on the Word of God, you can see yourself powerful and sturdy during times of weakness.

Therefore, when you are going through a time of weakness, never look at your circumstances from the outside with your natural eyes. Search the Word and find a Scripture that will give you hope, even if it doesn't look like anything is happening immediately. The main goal is to get out of the dilemma that is holding you in weakness and see yourself as strong.

If you are not strong you will stay in weakness too long bringing pity and uncertainty. We are not created to remain in a state of weakness because the longer we stay in that state; the longer we open ourselves up to negative attacks. This is why people often end up in ungodly relationships when they go through a season of weakness.

Someone may observe a person going through a trial and use that as a way to enter their lives with temptation. They inject sinful behavior into their lives by using their weakness to take advantage. During times of weakness, you must be careful of what you do and the company you keep. Many lives have been destroyed during times of weakness because one is not thinking properly, and anyone can seem like your savior. Therefore, you must always keep your spiritual eye open no matter how weak you are and find the Word.

Never be ashamed of your weaknesses; understand that everyone has them. If you are ashamed, there is nothing you or anyone else can do for you. You must want to seek help and deliverance in your weakness to be healed. Know that in time, you will overcome your weakness if you are patient and understanding with yourself. You must seek the answers for your own weakness. You might tell someone what your weakness is, but they may not feel what you do or experience what you do, so you must encourage yourself on and fight to be free. You will be better off fighting your own weakness.

For example, if you receive a bad report from a physician, instead of succumbing to the diagnosis and finding people who will throw you a pity party, use the Word to help you stay encouraged and remain strong. You may feel weak in the beginning, but over time you will get stronger.

Joshua 1:9 tells us: *"Have not I commanded thee? Be strong and of a good courage; be not afraid, neither be thou dismayed: for the Lord thy God is with thee whithersoever thou goest."* In all of your actions and weaknesses, you are never alone. Always know that God is with you. Always practice being strong and of good courage ahead of time so that when you are beset by weakness, you will be able to tackle your negative thoughts and behaviors. We all have weaknesses and we all have different methods of dealing with them. Conquer them with the Word and know that you are stronger than your greatest weakness.

CHAPTER 7

Rejecting the Flesh

Spiritually speaking, what exactly is the flesh? The flesh is that part of our being that operates out of our sinful nature. The flesh is stubborn, refuses correction, and does not want to listen. It hates to be under authority or yield to anything other than its own wishes. The flesh always wants what is forbidden; it is rebellious and unruly. No matter how you try to put the flesh under subjection, it will still try to do what it wants.

The flesh can cause many unwanted problems in your life if you allow it to get out of control. How many times have you seen a baby having a temper tantrum, kicking and screaming in an emotional tirade in search of whatever he wants? Just like babies, adults can have temper tantrums. When we don't get what we want, we emotionally spiral into a tantrum that can last for days.

When it comes to sexual temptation, the flesh can be antagonizing and unruly. How many relationships have been destroyed because a spouse or mate is not being satisfied in the flesh? The flesh may go on a hunt looking for someone to fulfill those desires, only to find that those desires can never truly be satisfied. The more the flesh gets, the more the flesh wants.

Galatians 5:16-19 tells us: *"This I say then, walk in the Spirit, and ye shall not fulfill the lust of the flesh. For the flesh lusteth against the Spirit, and the Spirit against the flesh: and these are contrary the one to the other: so that ye cannot do the things that ye would. But if ye led of the Spirit, ye are not under the law. Now the works of the flesh are manifest, which are these: adultery, fornication, uncleanness, lasciviousness."*

We walk in the flesh when we don't make a conscious effort to walk in the Spirit. Walking in the Spirit requires taking deliberate step-by-step motions in life, focusing on the Spirit within us, listening and doing His perfect will. When I think of walking, I think of a process in which we must take individual strides in order to reach a destination. The flesh is always trying to get you to slow down or stop walking in order to get you off course.

The flesh uses feelings and distractions to get you to focus on irrelevant things—anything other than the Spirit. The flesh can look at someone's outer characteristics and begin to engage in an emotional hunger that will leave you sexually attracted to someone forbidden.

We are constantly at war within ourselves; internally responding to what is right or wrong. Even when we think we are strong, we can find ourselves caught up in the flesh if we do not pay close attention. We must watch our flesh and keep it in check, as it must be tamed. Even the mind can cooperate with the flesh and have you lusting with mental erotic thoughts.

Romans 7:18 tells us: *"For I know that in me (That is in my flesh) dwelleth no good thing: for to will is present with me; but how to perform that which is good I find not."* In the flesh there is nothing good—even when you try to control the flesh, it can rebel at any time. This is why we should not get angry with our fleshly actions and thoughts, but instead learn how to control them.

People who find themselves in trouble of the flesh ignored their urges when they could have refocused them. When working with the flesh, we have to make the right judgments for everyone around us, as our fleshly actions not only involve us but others as well. Yes, it takes effort to stay the course, but the flesh should never overrule your emotions.

Romans 13:14 tells us: *"But put ye on the Lord Jesus Christ, and make not provision for the flesh, to fulfill the lust thereof."* The only thing that is powerful enough to conquer the flesh is the Lord Jesus Christ. We are commanded to put Him on so that we will make no provision for it. The flesh is so strong that nothing can tame it in this earthly realm.

Many people have turned to psychiatrists, and prayer warriors to help them successfully overcome their lustily sinful problems. Yet they find that their lust becomes even stronger as they spend time looking for cures. The more you reject the flesh, the more eager it is to rule. Once it is eager to rule, it can become dangerous if not controlled.

Galatians 6:8 tells us: *"For he that soweth to his flesh shall of the flesh reap corruption; but he that soweth to the Spirit shall of the Spirit reap life everlasting."* Who would deliberately sow into the flesh knowing that the end would be corruption? Yet there are many people sowing to the flesh and allowing the flesh to dictate their every move.

Being stigmatized as bearing a fleshly sin in a church setting can hurt one's reputation and chances of being promoted spiritually. People who are spiritually gifted but suffer secretly in sexual areas may never tell anyone because not enough compassion is given. They may feel forced to hide their erotic fantasy. We have yet to embrace those who suffer in sin and have allowed people to feel guilty about their imperfect lives. We should remember that all humans are imperfect and will, from time to time, experience temptation and desire

We should help those suffering to find deliverance and peace. They should not feel uncomfortable coming to other believers for help, if they are experiencing abnormal fleshly desires. If you are a believer you should be ready for any sexual sin that someone is bound in. You should not be afraid, scared that the spirit might jump on you. If you are real to the faith, your internal power is more than enough power to help those suffering.

Romans 8:7 tells us: *"Because the carnal mind is enmity against God: for it is not subject to the law of God, neither indeed can be."* This verse teaches us that the carnal or fleshly mind is an enemy against God. When you are always thinking in the flesh, it is impossible to live a good life. It is impossible to think right and heavenly things when the flesh is always grabbing at you. While living carnal or living of the flesh, you cannot obey the laws and the Words of the Bible. It is impossible to walk in the flesh and advance in greater spiritual progress. The flesh is constant and battles for your time and desires.

If you find the flesh controlling you and you have nowhere to turn, you need to take charge of your situation and start starving the flesh. Refusing to give into every command that it gives you. Reading the Word and rejecting those inner lewd feelings is the first step. Start with healing Scriptures as you can rehearse healing to yourself and speak words of encouragement.

Prayer and fasting helps to control the flesh and gives you the strength to reject what the flesh desires. At first, it may be hard to reject what the flesh is begging for, but after a few rejections, you will find that the flesh will calm down. Practicing this daily may be incredibly difficult but it *can* be done.

Learning what triggers your flesh also helps in maintaining control. If you have sexual weaknesses with certain individuals, you must stay away. You are asking for trouble if you allow your flesh to be around someone who entices you. For example, if you are weak when it comes to sexy men or women, make an effort to stay away from situations that would put you at risk in their presence.

You don't need a Bible to tell you that certain people and situations are not good for you when you are trying to overcome the flesh. We have to grow up spiritually if we want to be all that we are called to be and not be controlled by the flesh. You will automatically have a pull on your heart when your flesh is rising up, if you are a believer. You have to pay attention to yourself and know when to get yourself in order. Rise above the norm, and fight for your flesh.

John 8:7-11 tells us: *"So when they continued asking him, he lifted up himself, and said unto them, 'He that is without sin among you, let him first cast a stone at her.' And again he stooped down and wrote on the ground. And they which heard it, being convicted by their own conscience, went out one by one, beginning at the eldest, even unto the last: and Jesus was left alone, and the woman standing in the midst. When Jesus had lifted up himself and saw none but the woman, he said unto her, 'Woman where those are thine accusers: hath no man condemned thee?' She said, 'No man, Lord.' And Jesus said unto her, 'neither do I condemn thee: go and sin no more.'"*

It is interesting that the Scribes and Pharisees brought forth a woman who was caught in adultery and insisted that she be stoned. They pressed the issue because they knew if she was freed; the Law of Moses would not be upheld. But the law also required that the first stone be thrown by a person who is sinless in connection with the charge.

The accusers left one by one, from the oldest to the youngest, as there was no one sinless. We learn from this passage that we must not accuse others unless we search our own hearts and minds to make sure we are pure in every possible respect. We must be responsible for ourselves, and not be so eager to admonish someone else. It is easy to look at someone else's sin and make comments on how they need to change. But have you looked at your own sin? Sit and meditate on that question.

As we close out this chapter, we must remember to concentrate on rejecting the flesh. We should walk with our heads held high, knowing that no one can condemn us for our sins, as we have all fallen short at one time or another. Walking in the Spirit helps us to conquer the flesh, so we must get serious about walking in the Spirit. As we work to reject the flesh, we must be extra careful to transform our minds, moving from sinful thoughts into thoughts with integrity. This will, in turn, produce in us great men and women who are not walking in humiliation and flesh but in victory and success.

CHAPTER 8

Controlling Temptation

Never beat yourself down when you are tempted; realize that temptation is a part of life. You are not strange or possessed by demons because you are tempted; you are simply an imperfect human.

Temptation involves the flesh, body, and soul, so controlling temptation is going to take some effort. Instead of ignoring it and hoping it will go away, you must embrace it. If you are afraid of your temptations, you will have a hard time trying to control them. However, if you don't let your temptations intimidate you, then you can learn from them and control them.

Luke 22:40 tells us: *"And when he was at the place, he said unto them, pray that ye enter not into temptation."* Temptation is such a strong force that we must pray that we do not enter into it. We must be sincere in our prayers and want to keep ourselves from temptation. If temptation was something that we could ignore without help, then no one would be tempted. But because we are fleshly sexual beings, we need Heavenly help to keep us safe.

We will always be tempted by something sexually. You might be tempted to look at that unholy picture or to call that person you just met. However, it is how you react to the temptation that determines your ultimate failure or victory.

Two tempted people in the same situation is a disaster waiting to happen. How many people are in jail now because they were tempted to a night of passion and their desire overtook them? How many people are divorced because they allowed their temptations to overtake them? Although neither of these situations may describe your personal temptations, there is surely something that has tempted you and caused you trouble.

We spend considerable time on our looks, our talents, and our assets so that people can recognize us. But do we ever think of our daily walk and daily bouts of temptation? Our flesh is always with us, so why don't we take care and manage our fleshly temptations like we pay heed to our outer appearances? All our materialistic possessions will mean nothing if we cannot control the flesh and walk in respect for ourselves and others. The flesh does not care how much money you have or what car you drive. No matter who you are, your flesh can rise up and act out at any time following a temptation.

This is why you should be ready, alert, and never surprised. If you are agonizing over certain temptations, stop and prepare yourself to face them. If you admit that you have temptations and make an effort to understand them, you can be ready with a plan. For example, if you have a tendency to be tempted by any man or woman who approaches you in a sexual manner, then you need to work on transforming your mind when it comes to certain conversations which may lead you down a path of sexual immorality.

A woman whom we will call Marina learned that temptation can be a powerful unwanted force. Marina put her career ahead of her personal life for years; she was forty-five by the time she was ready for marriage. When she started dating, she never could find a man who lived up to her personal standards and ran away men who were close.

In her search for a companion, Marina felt frustrated and alone because nothing turned out right in her relationships. She continued living a lonely life and gave up on any type of love. After several years of trying to date, Marina started living like an old maid, wearing the same pajamas daily and not keeping herself groomed properly.

One day at work, Marina met a man who came into her office to drop off a package. This individual, whom we will call Roman, was the first man in years to pay her some attention. He was straightforward and rugged, and he was clear in his affections toward her, always telling her how beautiful she was. Marina noticed that Roman always dropped off packages on Monday, so every Monday she would wear extra makeup and tight clothing, knowing that she would see him.

One Monday, Marina set out to be the only person in the office when Roman arrived. When he came in, he flirted as usual and Marina enjoyed every moment. As Roman kept flirting, he finally moved toward the real reason he was there: "Give me a quickie," he said. Roman started undressing in front of Marina right in the office; she felt weak and out of control. She was so tempted that she started crying, as she knew that she should stop and send him on his way.

She hesitated for a moment but kept looking at his strong muscular body and was unable to resist. In thirty seconds flat, Marina had all of her clothes off and was in the corner office having sex with a man whom she barely knew. After fifteen minutes of passion, Roman exited the office, leaving Marina to clean up the mess.

Marina was still on an emotional high three weeks after her episode, looking out the window, excited to see Roman. Her behavior changed; now she was always joyful and excited to be at work. This made the other employees suspicious, as they knew that Marina always complained about anything she could.

One day while on the phone at work, Marina started telling a friend about her "one-day stand" with the delivery man. She was giggling and running her hands through her hair as if he was right there. She did not know that a coworker was listening to her conversation and taking notice of her behavior, intending to expose her.

A month after Marina's phone conversation, she was told to see her supervisor. She knew something was wrong because the supervisor was not stationed at her location. Marina was told that they had been watching her on the camera on a certain Monday and had received complaints about her behavior from the business next door. She knew this was a lie but it was nothing she could do. Marina was shown the recording and was intensely embarrassed when she saw herself running around the office naked with Roman. Marina tried everything she could to keep her job, including filing a privacy-related lawsuit, but later resigned due to embarrassment.

After Marina resigned, she set out to investigate Roman. She found that he had been intimate with several women at offices where he delivered packages. Marina never saw Roman again, although she made several attempts to find him. She was terribly upset with herself and could not understand why she could not control her temptations. In intense physical and mental pain, she turned against herself, blaming herself for the mess her life had become. Eventually, she became so stressed that she ended up spending several months in a mental institution.

What if Marina had refused to take the bait of temptation and held out from any sexual connection? She would still have a job and a chance for a prosperous life. Marina's story is not all that unique; we all know someone who has experienced a similar situation having a sexual connection at work that turns out to be a setback.

The challenge is stopping temptation before it begins. Although temptation can seem so innocent, the Enemy never shows you the expected end that is already set. Roman couldn't have cared less about Marina, but in her mind, he was the best thing that ever happened. And that's how the temptation won out over her better judgment.

1st Thessalonians 4:4-5 reminds us: "*That every one of you should know how to possess his vessel in sanctification and honor; not in the lust of concupiscence, even as the Gentiles which know not God.*" In our moments of weakness, we should know how to purify ourselves in sanctification. Although it feels hard when we're being tempted, we should not let our behavior be controlled by desperation and loneliness.

Concupiscence is a strong desire, especially sexual desire, as we should not act like the Gentiles. We should be aware of our behavior and know that we should be stronger than temptation. Marina knew at the onset of her temptation that it was wrong. That split second of hesitation was her chance to get out. But the Tempter makes it very difficult for us to do the right thing as he pressures us and forces us to conform to the ways of the flesh.

That split second is where we all fail. We know when something is wrong but in our weakness, it is hard to resist. Yet we must learn how to resist because temptation is never good. I have never spoken to anyone who fell into temptation and later told me that it was the best thing that ever happened to them.

1st Corinthians 10:13 tells us: *"There hath no temptation taken you but such as is common to man: but God is faithful , who will not suffer you to be tempted above that ye are able; but will with the temptation also make a way to escape, that ye may be able to bear it."* Isn't it good to know that there is nothing that can overtake us that we cannot escape? We all have an alarming story of temptation that we can tell, but we are not left alone to combat the Tempter that comes to steal our joy.

When you are low and struggling with temptation, remember that there is always a way out. Remember to read the Word and always see yourself as a victor and not a victim as you find ways to be conscious of your environment and safely exit all forms of temptation.

CHAPTER 9

A Foul Spirit

When I think of the word foul, I think of a bad odor permeating the air. It's like dropping a piece of raw meat into a crack in the kitchen and smelling a foul odor after several days. Sometimes it takes a while to find the source, but the foul smell guides you to the trapped meat. Once you have found and destroyed the decaying meat, the odor goes away.

Similarly, you might encounter a foul spirit. A foul spirit emerges when a person's attitude is unclean, impure, and wicked. You can tell by the words that a person speaks if they have a foul spirit. For example, if they are always eager to tell dirty jokes, or to talk about sexual and impure activities, you can rest assured they have a foul spirit. But just like the meat in the kitchen, you can't always recognize a foul spirit in a person right away. It may take several conversations before you realize their foulness.

After you recognize a foul spirit in someone, it is up to you to remove yourself from the situation. If you stay around someone with a foul spirit long enough, you will start acting and smelling like them. You must remove yourself before the odor clings to you.

You can have a foul, lustful spirit and not even know it. This spirit often enters when you are going through difficult times. This is why it is important for you to watch yourself during your times of weakness and choose the right friendships, ones that encourage you with positive thoughts.

The hardest times in life confront you with personal problems and weakness. This is when you start straying away from the things of God and going your own way. Your flesh starts to get hungry as you open yourself up to activities and events that entertain foulness. This type of spirit can take years or even a lifetime to conquer.

We can find an example of this foul spirit in the life of Tommy, who almost slipped into utter ruin. Tommy was a believer, but he fell on hard times after his wife filed for a divorce. He moved out of his home and started a new job in Manhattan working with people of different religions and cultures. He befriended many on the job, assuming that his popularity would help him get the promotion he so badly wanted. A promotion would mean more money to support himself apart from his wife. It would also help him improve his reputation, which his wife continued to bash.

Tommy didn't realize that his behavior was slowly changing as he started hanging around single women at work and going to happy hour from time to time. Sometimes he would get home at two in the morning, wake up late for work, and have a hard time drying out from a night of drinking.

This went on for months as Tommy experienced a false sense of excitement, feeling happier and more accepted by his friends. Tommy started going to X-rated movies with coworkers and filled the rest of the night with clubbing. His former wife would call and ask him to spend time with his two children, as she was beginning to be overwhelmed by raising them by herself. Tommy would ignore her calls and keep living his life as a single man, enjoying X-rated movies and drinking.

Tommy's friends made his situation worse by tempting him with women and laughing at his destructive behavior. He would often have one-night stands and feel no remorse for his behavior, labeling it as fun. After a year of this, Tommy found himself tempted to buy dirty magazines, encouraged by his "friends." He would wake up early, put on sunglasses, and buy the magazines from neighborhood stores. Focusing on the magazines made him forget his horrible divorce and need for intimacy.

Tommy later found himself masturbating while reading the magazines and falling deeper into foulness. He told himself that his behavior was okay because he was lonely and stressed from his divorce. He became obsessed with dirty magazines, even placing them in his car for his commute. His thoughts became more bizarre and disordered; he began stopping in adult stores and staying there for hours as the clubs weren't satisfying his sexual needs. Tommy's foul spirit was getting unbearable and out of his control.

One day, Tommy drove to an adult store from work and ran into a member of his church lurking at the checkout counter holding a Gospel pamphlet. Being embarrassed, he tried to ignore the man, but the man recognized him and spoke to him.

As Tommy conversed with this man, he felt an inward shame come upon him and suddenly realized what was going on. He had so many tapes and books that they were falling out of his hands. As all of his tapes fell, it was like a light went off in Tommy's head. He realized that he had been overtaken by a foul and lustful spirit—a spirit that was controlling him and driving him to do things that he would not normally do. Tommy then felt a presence of peace, something he had not felt in a long time, as he was trying to cut the conversation short.

As Tommy was talking to the unknown man in the store, he was not truly paying attention. His mind was revisiting all the events of the past year and how he had been laying with strange women and literally corrupting his life. Tommy was embarrassed but glad that he had run into another believer.

As Tommy drove home, he felt like he was on the outside looking at his life. He had neglected his children and treated his former wife like a piece of trash. All of his bad behaviors were running through his mind as he realized that foulness was directing him, and he had to do something about it. Tommy kept thinking about the man at the store and how he was an angel sent to him for deliverance. Although he was ready for healing, the lustful thoughts still tormented him and begged him to come back.

From that day, it took Tommy years to get back in order as he went through several trials. He was not promoted because of another employee who was spreading malicious rumors about him. He had to report to court several times to prove that he had not fathered the child of a woman with whom he'd had a one-night stand. He also had to report to the court on another case, as one of his intimate partners was under aged. Meanwhile, his divorce was settled however, he still had drama associated with it. Tommy was threatened with jail several times during that season of his life, but grace kept him free. A foul and lustful spirit almost ruined him, but he survived.

Revelation 18:2 tells us: *"And he cried mightily with a strong voice, saying 'Babylon the great is fallen, is fallen and is become the habitation of devils, and the hold of every foul spirit, and a cage of every unclean and hateful bird.'"*

Foul and lustful spirits need a special environment to permeate and operate. Your spirit must be open to allow nasty thoughts to come in and infiltrate your thinking. In Revelation, a voice cried out that Babylon the great had fallen. When foul spirits take over a territory, other negative and unclean things can also invade.

This is why you should watch your thoughts and your surroundings when you are up against a foul spirit. You must make sure you are not being dragged into dirty activity which can later create a mountain of corruption. As Tommy would testify, his foul spirit became stronger as his environment opened, enabling more exotic and lustful sins to occur.

James 1:21 tells us: *"Wherefore lay apart all filthiness and superfluity of naughtiness, and receive with meekness the engrafted word, which is able to save your souls."* This passage in James tells us to "lay apart all filthiness." This means we must make an effort to lay it down and step away. Foulness and filthiness can occur both inside and outside. Our internal thoughts and feelings will manifest itself outwardly in time.

In order to live a prosperous life, we must receive the Word with meekness, which heals and delivers us from all of our filthy sins and desires. Remember that a foul spirit can sneak up on you at any time. Your environment and the company around you influence how filthy your thoughts might be. Being aware of those around you and what you watch and hear is important.

So be wise and steadfast when dealing with a foul spirit and know that having a clean spirit not only gives you peace but gives you a good indication that you are following the Word. When you follow the Word, you will not have the room to fill your life with other foul items. You too can have peace and stability in knowing that a foul spirit can be overcome, but you must be willing to receive help and fight for your freedom and not be held captive.

CHAPTER 10

The Shame Connection

Any time we get caught up in temptation, there is a shame connection. Although we may not admit it, we feel a sense of humiliation that follows us. We also have to live with the shame that the world passes on to us and never lets us forget. Even if others forget our shame, we often put shame on ourselves.

Have you noticed that the world waits until you become successful before exposing your sins and tempting ways? As long as you are poor and asking others for money, no one says anything. It's only when you become successful that others want to dig up your past and accuse you of temptation. They spend hours looking at your life, as they would love for you to bow your head down and fall into condemnation because of past mistakes.

The world seems to experience joy when they find a Christian with a shameful past. As long as you are not a Christian, you can walk around speaking heresy and committing shameful acts, but if you are a Christian doing those same things, it won't be long before someone recognizes you and displays your entire life for everyone to see.

It's only when the believer believes the lies and walks around in humiliation that the accusers have won in their accusations. Believers are to never walk in humiliation or embarrassment no matter what the situation. We must be strong in the Lord and in the power of His might.

Isaiah 54:4 tells us: *"Fear not; for thou shalt not be ashamed: neither be thou confounded; for thou shalt not be put to shame: for thou shalt forget the shame of thy youth, and shalt not remember the reproach of thy widowhood anymore."* There are Scriptures in the Bible that reminds us that we should not be ashamed because shame brings on fear and distress. We may fear gossip or what people are going to say about us, or fear that we cannot take the shame. As believers, we must stop being ashamed and allowing the spirit of shame to control us. All someone needs to do is to spread a nasty lie or rumor and we walk around in shame—even when the rumor is untrue. We often worry about our reputations and how people perceive us.

A man whom we'll call Kenny learned from his mistakes about the shame connection. On Kenny's fortieth birthday, he made a bet with himself that he would find a good wife by the end of the year. His nights were lonely, as he was a self-made millionaire who had no one to spend his money on. Kenny was always afraid to talk about his money, as he thought women would only date him for his financial status and not for who he was. He also had an aggressive tone of voice and would often drive women away with his outspoken nature, which often attracted others' attention.

One night while visiting a jazz club, Kenny had his eyes on one lady who appeared interested in his pickup lines. This woman, whom we'll call Cherry, appeared sincere and talked with Kenny all night. She told Kenny that she was from Brazil and she was only in the country for a while looking for a school to attend. Kenny enjoyed her company and saw an opportunity for love as she laughed with him the entire night.

After exchanging numbers, Kenny formed a good and respectful relationship with Cherry that felt real and wholehearted. Kenny called his married friends and told them that he had finally found love in his life of madness. Kenny and Cherry dated for months, and Kenny wasted no time getting his life in order for marriage.

Cherry saw that Kenny was getting serious, but she didn't care, as she wasn't looking for a serious relationship at the time. Kenny finally felt complete as he knew that Cherry loved him, even though she didn't show any signs.

Kenny finally decided to pop the question after doing considerable soul searching. Although he didn't know much about Cherry, he was ready for marriage. He set his proposal day on a Friday, as he had met Cherry at the jazz club on a Friday. Kenny packed an engagement ring and a new outfit, and then asked Cherry to meet him at his beach house, as they would often meet at his second home. Cherry had her own key and would always be at the house waiting for him. Kenny's adrenaline was pumping as he was speeding on the way to meet Cherry. When he arrived, he was surprised to see blue balloons in the driveway, which led him to believe that Cherry had a surprise for him.

As Kenny let himself in the beach house, he noticed that the lock was loose instead of strong and secure. When he opened the door, he saw everything in his upscale house gone, even the bathroom pipes. His heart was broken to pieces and he was embarrassed.

After filing a report and looking at the security camera, Kenny saw Cherry and the two men she claimed to be her cousins robbing his house. Kenny started crying as he saw Cherry running through his house on camera with his expensive jewelry.

After some thought, Kenny realized there were signs of danger he should have recognized; Cherry was always asking about him, but never revealed anything about herself. He realized that he was so desperate for a woman that he lost all sense of reality and was living in a fantasy world that ultimately cost him more than $100,000.

Kenny finally realized that Cherry had been watching him at the jazz club and knew that he had money. He became ashamed and depressed and would only go to bars and football games for comfort.

He started missing church services, as he thought that people were judging him, even though they knew nothing about his situation. Kenny never told anyone about his loss of love or his financial loss, as he had been told that there was a string of women robbing men in the city. The worst part of Kenny's story was that he was still in love with Cherry and fighting internally to get her off his mind.

Kenny tried to find peace by joining a church ministry for men. But after he told his story he felt like they were judging his decisions, and labelling him as a fool.

There are people now sitting at home who have vowed never to walk into a church again due to a bout with shame. Someone said something or noticed something and made them feel ashamed or embarrassed.

Religious people or people who hate caused them to tear apart their desire to do the work of the Kingdom, simply because they may have made a mistake that caused them shame or condemnation. Often people with shame assume that others know about their situations when actuality they know nothing. This is why they stay distant from people and try to heal themselves in solitary.

Let's take someone who has been to prison for years. When they return to church or to our community do we stare and wonder what they went to prison for? Or do we embrace them to help them return back to society as a productive person?

Can they sense that you are trying to keep them condemned, and judge them for what they have done? Yes there are many Christians who have been to prison for crimes. However they should not be afraid to return back to church wondering how they will be perceived by their church community.

Yes, we should be careful about criminal activity and careful about those who are a part of it; however those who are genuine in changing should be welcomed and given an opportunity to repent and change their lives. We must do better when it comes to the least the lost and the left out.

Philippians 3:13-14 it tells us: *"Brethren, I count not myself to have apprehended: but this one thing I do, forgetting those things which are behind, and reaching forth unto those things which are before. I press toward the mark for the prize of the high calling of God in Christ Jesus."* As these verses tell us, we must forget those things that are behind us. The Enemy of our soul wants us to constantly live in condemnation and be regretful for the past pains we put on others. He often reminds us in our good times of how terrible we used to be, so that we can never advance in physical and emotional prosperity.

It is only when we are true to ourselves and take responsibility for our decisions that we can fully be ready for healing from our shame. Shame not only affects us, but it affects others around us as well. We must press toward the mark, which means leaving our shame behind and moving forward toward greatness.

No one great was given anything; they had to toil and constantly work toward their goals. Most great men and women spent years learning and studying their trades and refusing to go down roads of shame.

As long as you are sitting in shame and self-pity, you will stay where you are, waiting on someone else to rescue you. If you get up and follow the Scripture of Philippians and get motivated, you will find that moving toward the mark will ease the pain of your past and help you forget your shameful mistakes.

Shame often comes alongside blaming someone or something for your failings. Let's examine the situation of an adult who acts like a juvenile. Every time he is caught in something, it's always, "It was my father who was never there"; "It was my teacher who hated me!" The blame game is always at the front—it was always someone else's fault. Others may have affected your life, but there comes a time when you have to take responsibility for yourself and get well in areas where you are ashamed and hiding.

We all have shame and blame that we can use against others. But we live in an imperfect world and we live with imperfect people. There will always be situations in which we miss the mark and feel some form of shame, but you must not allow these feeling to last in your heart.

Isaiah 50:7 is a good verse to meditate on in your times of shame. This verse tells us: *"For the Lord God will help me; therefore shall I not be confounded: therefore have I set my face like a flint, and I know that I shall not be ashamed."* Sometimes we have to read a verse over and over until we can see it in our heart. As we overcome our mistakes and shame, we need the Word as an advocate to drive us into thinking more positively about ourselves.

Rina's story tells us about someone who battled the shame connection. Rina did not have a boyfriend or close friend for over ten years. She was very self-conscious of her weight and decided that she would not date anyone until she lost one hundred pounds. On one down day, Rina met an old friend whom we will call Will. After exchanging numbers, Rina called Will the same night. After meeting with Will several days later, Rina fell into temptation and made the mistake of sleeping with him in desperation. Her lack of companionship made her extra vulnerable to any man that came along.

After her one-night stand with Will, though, Rina found herself being blackmailed. She received pictures of her obese naked body in compromising positions with a note attached that said, "Dummy give me ten thousand dollars or else." Rina was so devastated and ashamed that she paid the money and never told anyone about her ordeal.

She later found out that Will was traveling to different cities, looking up old friends and running the same con. Knowing that other women had suffered from the same scam made her feel better as she thought she was his only victim. She remained in a state of shock because she felt she was too good to be deceived by anyone. Her shame still lasts to this day, as she has never trusted a man and decided to live her life free from dating and marriage. In her stress and loneliness Rina gained another one hundred pounds worrying about her relationships with men.

As we can see from Rina's experience, temptation is closely related to shame. Once you fall into temptation, you have no after effects of the situation. Never let yourself get caught off guard by living a discouraged life, putting yourself in a situation where someone can take advantage of you, and cause you humiliation. We all are created with worth no matter what color or size we may be. We must know our self-worth so that others can see our positive attitude and not make us a victim based on our behavior.

Hebrews 4:16 tells us: *"Let us therefore come boldly unto the throne of grace that we may obtain mercy, and find grace to help in time of need."* This Scripture tells us that we can go boldly before the throne of grace. Grace is something that we all need; it is unmerited favor. When we face shame, it is hard for us to move past our behavior, regroup, and know that we are entitled to grace.

Shame tries to latch onto us and make our way heavy. People in shame hold their heads down assuming that others know the details of their wrongdoings. Only the Cross has allowed mercy and grace in our times of need. We should always be grateful that Jesus has covered our shame and given us the grace that we need so desperately.

CHAPTER 11

Recalling Righteousness

In order to be successful in anything you do spiritually, you must first recall your righteousness. We have already been declared righteous; therefore we must walk in it. The Cross is the most important mission of the Bible, so we must remember what it took to make us righteous. The least we can do for Christ, who suffered so that we could reconcile with God Almighty, is to conduct ourselves in a righteous way.

Although we will never be perfect, we should respect ourselves and not come off as filthy sinners for the unbeliever to scoff at. We should be witnesses and people of faith who are able to control our carnal desires and emotions.

When a believer has many known gifts and talents, and falls into sexual temptation, they become like a balloon that is released from a hand. It goes up slowly at first, but it's not before long the balloon is out of sight. Such fallen believers lose the approval of the people and chase away good friendships.

However, those who have been tested in this area should not be overly hard on themselves, but must understand that we are all born into sin. We must be grateful that we have an Advocate who understands our weaknesses and sinful actions and still intercedes for us.

This is why we must not panic when we fall into sexual sins. When we commit sexual sin, we disrespect ourselves and somehow feel inadequate and unrighteous. People who live in sin often disregard church and live in condemnation, sorrow, or apathy. They feel guilty and begin to be rebellious against the faith.

But you should not let your sinful behaviors interfere with your spiritual life and start you on a path to nowhere. Nothing is a surprise to our Father. This is why Jesus came to the earth; He knew that we would all need help in our sinful states and that we cannot do it on our own.

Romans 12:1 tells us: "*I beseech you therefore, brethren, by the mercies of God, that ye present your bodies a living sacrifice, holy, acceptable unto God, which is your reasonable service.*" Our bodies must be a living sacrifice so that we can reach the world whenever and wherever we are needed. If we are living in sin, it is hard for us to be witnesses and hard for others to come to know the Gospel through us.

We should try not to commit the same spiritual infractions as heartless sinners because our souls have been bought with a price. Being a living sacrifice, of course, is not an easy task. It is only through the Holy Spirit that we are able to follow the commands of the Bible in a way that is pleasing. If we only knew what it took for us to get to this point, we would be more than grateful to be living sacrifices.

Of course, we all have up and down moments, but we have a Savior who is willing to help us with sin in every aspect of our lives. John 14:17-18 tells us: *"Even the Spirit of truth, whom the world cannot receive, because it seeth him not, neither knoweth him: but ye know him; for he dwelleth with you, and shall be in you: I will not leave you comfortless: I will come to you."* This is the best-kept secret in our faith: He will not leave us comfortless.

When we fall, we feel embarrassed and hide our sins, throwing pity parties for ourselves behind closed doors. Instead, we must realize that we have a Comforter who is willing to help us overcome our daily challenges and struggles by staying in us and reminding us of His Word. Matthew 6:33 tells us: *"But seek ye first the kingdom of God, and his righteousness, and all these things shall be added unto you."* Often, when we go through hard times, instead of seeking the Kingdom and the Word, we start forming our own ideas and trying to solve our own problems. Our pride often gets in the way as we become impatient, trying to force things to happen. We call others to gripe about our problems and gossip about our situations. However, when we seek the Kingdom first, we are doing what the Bible tells us to do. Thus, we should expect all things will be added unto us.

I am reminded of a lady whom we will call Phyllis. Phyllis was living a good and prosperous life. She had a husband and a child, and they had two incomes, which provided them a comfortable life. Phyllis's problem was her routine. She was bored with the same old routine and found herself looking for something she thought was her purpose. She did not feel fulfilled by anyone or anything in her life, so she assumed something was missing. She tried out various evening activities and tried to make new friends, but her daily routine made it hard for her to get out regularly.

Phyllis enrolled in evening school, assuming that a new class would help her get excited about life. While in school, she made several friends, but she realized that she was much older and more mature, so she kept her distance while learning and striving to obtain a degree. As time went on, Phyllis realized that enrolling in school was not the answer to her problems and began to struggle with balancing classwork and home life. She felt moody and unstable as school and home became overwhelming.

One day during a break in class, Phyllis met a man whom we will call Pete. He seemed to be interested in her boring life. After he found out everything about her, Pete managed to tempt her into an intimate relationship with him. He began pulling her away from her home life, competing with her husband by demanding more of her time.

Phyllis was excited when her illicit relationship first began because the secrecy of sneaking around kept her on an emotional high. Someone other than her husband was giving her attention, which introduced more excitement into her life.

After months of infidelity, Phyllis realized that Pete was getting careless by calling her at night and following her home. Phyllis was so stressed out about her husband finding out about her boyfriend that she began losing her hair and losing weight. Her appearance became so different that people started asking if she was sick. She would often look out the window at home, checking to see if her boyfriend was stalking her. Every time she heard a sound, she assumed that Pete was sitting outside of her home, watching.

After experiencing insomnia, migraines, and a trip to the emergency room, Phyllis finally came to herself like the prodigal son in Luke. She asked herself, "What am I doing?" It was like looking at another person. She was devastated when a friend told her she looked like a character in *The Walking Dead*, but somehow, she was able to see herself for who she had become. Sin had taken over and had made her into a different person. She realized how far she had gone and began to take her life back.

Phyllis started going back to church, where she would always get a good Word. She started praying and seeking help and stopped seeing herself as an unproductive woman who had no purpose. She saw herself as righteous despite how she looked or felt.

After several weeks of prayer and healing, Phyllis called Pete and cut him off completely. She had a new attitude and enrolled at a school closer to her home. She noticed that her life was getting better; she received better grades and her company gave her a supervisory position. It was not easy for Phyllis, but she made up her mind to do better each day.

Phyllis's story ended well because she understood that her sin had taken her all the way down, and she knew she had to do something about it—especially when it was going to affect others in her life. Phyllis was fortunate because not all sinful situations have a happy ending. She was grateful that everything worked out in her favor, especially looking back at her wretched and sinful life. She was sucked into temptation due to routine and boredom.

Perhaps you are in the same situation as Phyllis, living a double life. You are putting on a show for the world to see, pretending to be a family person but living an entirely different life between the sheets.

Just like Phyllis there is hope for you, and you don't have to live like that. You must step back and see yourself and recognize what you are doing. Just know that you are special, and you should treat yourself as someone special. It is only then; you can recognize how far sin has taken you and do something about it.

Sin will never stop on its own without resistance. Remember righteousness and what it took for you to be righteous. Know that if you turn back from your sins and repent, you can move forward and put those sinful activities behind. Our Righteousness comes through Jesus and the Cross. We must be grateful that He was obedient in His assignment and made a way for us to claim our righteousness through Him.

CHAPTER 12

Staying Focused

I f you are serious about conquering temptation, you must stay focused and put time into the process. You must say to yourself "I can do this! When I think of staying focused, I think all of the major athletes who spend years perfecting their sport and becoming experts in their field.

While others are partying and having fun, they are practicing their form and staying fit. Staying focused and on task is the one thing that sets them apart. They know the prize of greatness awaits them in the end, and they fight to accomplish their goals. They find the time to apply discipline in the areas in which they are great, and in the areas where they are weak, they spend time building up their strength.

You must think like an athlete and stay focused on the task at hand when it comes to temptation. Ironically, sexual temptation is something you must stay focused on in order to stay away. You cannot assume that you are so anointed and talented that you will never fall into temptation. Just like an athlete, you must study and practice in order to break the binding powers of temptation.

When you are anointed for a purpose, you can look so appealing to others that they will go out of their way to entice you and get you tied up in a web of temptation. The Enemy's job is to kill your desire to serve your purpose, and have you tied up in unnecessary desires. Not paying attention and getting distracted can take us off course and have us thirsty in unnecessary desires.

Matthew 5:14 tells us: *"Ye are the light of the world; a city that is set on a hill cannot be hid."* You are always noticeable, and will stand out as a Christian even if you are not trying to. There is something about you that makes people wonder, because you are anointed. They don't care what the heathens or the backbiters are doing—but when it comes to you; they are watching and waiting to see what you will do next.

This is why you must protect yourself and your anointing. It is not easy being a Christian in this day and time, because you must watch the motives and intentions of people around you. You don't have to walk around suspicious of everyone, but as a Christian, you are expected to watch out for those who would intentionally entrap you in areas of temptation in order to stop you from fulfilling your destiny.

Yes! Christians are expected to be good people, and people who encourage others in the Gospel, but we should not be so religious that we don't see the Enemy when he comes to attack and tempt us. You must maintain your primary focus on the works of the Gospel, but place a secondary focus on keeping yourself alert to the tricks of people who do not want you to succeed.

The world watches believers and holds us to a higher standard than the rest. This means that believers must always be ready and focused on a task. We are examples for the world to follow, so we should always be alert and watching ourselves, lest we fall into temptation.

Unfortunately, it is an ugly world out there and you must fight in the Spirit with your sword of the Word to maintain a sense of self-denial and keep your emotional thoughts from getting out of hand. The humanistic side of you will always scream, "I want some love!" But you must stay strong and think rationally. Yes, as a Christian you can be starving for love, but you must not let your starvation take control, because it will make you a target.

Colossians 3:2 tells us: *"Set your affection on things above, not on things on this earth."* In your weakest hour think on things above. This does not mean to set your affection above others and move around like you are better than others, throwing religion around like a weapon. Instead, this passage means that you must set your affection on things above, looking to Heaven and the Word for your answers and concerns. Staying focused involves intention and patience in all situations even when you are having difficult times. You must be so focused that you are ready for any situation that comes your way. It can be hard in this day and age because there are so many outside distractions that can take your focus away, but such discipline is essential.

We should not walk around scared and uncertain about what may come our way. Yes, it can be frightening trying to overcome certain temptations. But if we learn to stay focused on the Word, we will be ready when temptation inevitably comes, and we will overcome the pitfalls that come our way.

We must know that our lives have a greater cause than living a simple routine. Good standing and right behavior are things that we must strive for; they will not be handed to us. We must educate ourselves and stay alert in our times of testing and be mindful of everything we do.

John 14:27 tells us: *"Peace I leave with you, my peace I give unto you: not as the world giveth, give I unto you. Let not your heart be troubled, neither let it be afraid."* Peace is the answer to all the situations that we face. When we are tempted, our peace is compromised; therefore, we lose focus. Once our focus is lost we will be open for anything that is brought to us.

As we understand our temptation, reject it, and do the right things, we will find that our focus will be better, and we can rest knowing that peace will guide us into freedom. As we read the Word, we come to understand that peace has been given to us. This allows us to live upright lives and do battle to overcome sexual temptation in stillness knowing that we can overcome.

It is up to us to maintain our focus and engage in battle if we want to live above sexual temptation and overcome our overzealous desires. It is not our job to stay mad with tempters and spend our lives hating on people who try to destroy us sexually. But is our job to learn how to deal with each situation as it comes and find the right way of finding harmony in moving past unwanted seductions and attractions.

The good thing is we have everything we need to assist us in accomplishing this goal. Reading the Word, praying, and being alert to our surroundings are just a few strategies we explored throughout each chapter of this book.

Although we have these tools to guide us, it is essential that we remain consistent in our efforts, as temptation is a force that will never go away. Of course, we will make mistakes, because we are all imperfect in an imperfect world. However, we don't have to dwell on our mistakes and make a mockery of our lives chasing temptations.

This book was written to help you focus on the right things, those which are required to maintain a sense of self-dignity as we seek ways to conquer sexual temptation and escape its grip. Sexual temptation is not a joke or something we should ignore. It is a real urge that can come and destroy anyone's life.

Just as you work a job from nine to five, you need to stay focused on sexual temptation from nine to five—and far beyond. If you don't and make one wrong move, following your temptations, your life can be altered forever.

Yes, we all have sexual desires and we all have days where we are weaker in some respects. But allowing yourself to become so weak that you let your temptations overtake you and cast you into a spiritual ditch can be a catastrophe. Remember: It is up to you to control yourself and your thoughts, and to live your life to the best of your ability.

So refrain from these urges that can ultimately destroy you and all you have worked for. Fight for your dignity and use the tools that you have been given in this book. Remember to be wise as a serpent in all that you do, and keep watch, knowing that sexual temptation is only confronting you to destroy you—but wisdom, understanding, and our Savior holds the key to an upright and redeemed life!

BATTLING SEXAUL TEMPTATION?

If you are battling sexual temptation and it's overtaking your life, try Jesus!

Repeat this prayer:

Dear Jesus, I come to you admitting that I am battling sexual temptations. I come to you with a sincere heart as I confess you as my Lord and Savior. I believe that you died on the Cross and rose again with all power in your hands. This includes the power to break me free from my unnatural sexual desires and the emotional pain that often overtakes me. Thank you, Lord, for your healing power, as the Cross is healing me. Thank you for saving me, and for receiving me into the Kingdom. I will forever be grateful for your love toward me.

About Sheela Fields

Sheela Fields is a baptized believer who focuses on debatable subjects such as sexual sins and repulsive iniquities. She is a catalyst for intercession and prayer and believes that all believers should desire spiritual gifts such as healing, prophecy, and the working of miracles.

She believes that the church is the most powerful entity on earth, in which true believers are united for one purpose. Her motto is, "There is nothing that cannot be accomplished when faith, belief, and the prayer of the righteous connect."

She is a graduate of Tuskegee University in Alabama where she graduated with a Degree in Business Administration. She resides in Ft. Lauderdale, Florida and has one son.

www.ingramcontent.com/pod-product-compliance
Lightning Source LLC
LaVergne TN
LVHW051811080426
835513LV00017B/1900